CONVICTED

What to expect and how to make it through a federal prison sentence

R. D. Mcilwain

First Edition

Acknowledgments

First of all I would like to thank my Lord and Savior Jesus Christ for giving me the strength and ability to write about my past experiences.. I'm also thankful for the opportunity to use what I've been through to give comfort and clarity to others..

I would also like to thank my parents; Peggy McIlwain and Glenn Wilfong for never giving up on me. Special thanks to S. Forrest (smile) for helping me and countless others reach our FULL potential. You truly have a gift!

About the Author

R.D. Mcilwain is an author, speaker, mentor and entrepreneur. He served 12 years in the federal prison system for a drug offense. During his incarceration, Mr. McIlwain overcame his circumstances through: faith in God and by diligently educating himself.

Mr. McIlwain attended college (business management), became a certified personal trainer, and authored 3 books; all while in prison. He is now dedicated to mentoring and helping others reach their full physical, mental, and spiritual potential.

Contents

Introduction

If you're reading this book, chances are you or someone you care about is on the way to federal prison........

From personal experience, I have a pretty good idea of what you're going through. I know your mind isn't at peace and that you're dealing with many stressful emotions. Especially if you've never experienced a situation such as this. At the moment you're probably feeling at least one of the following:

Anger – angry with yourself, or those that contributed to your current circumstances.

Anxiety – constantly worried about what your family will do without you. Probably not sleeping well either.

Depression – because life is about to drastically change from what you and your family is accustomed to.

Fear – probably terrified about what you might face on the inside. By now you've heard all the horror stories about what takes place in prison- fights, homosexuality, extortion, killings, etc.

Frustration – it seems as if you have no control over whats happening in your life right now.

Hurt – some of the people that you care about have turned their backs on you. Or simply treat you like an outcast.

Shock – never in your wildest dreams did you think that you'd be on your way to prison!!

If any of these thoughts and emotions have weighed heavily on your mind and heart lately; don't feel bad my friend. You have every right to feel and think these things. This is a major turning point in your life; but its not the end. Many others (myself included) have been in the same position you're in now, and we made it through. There's no reason whatsoever that you can't do the same.

Before we move on, I must first be brutally honest with you. I **cannot** tell you that "everything will be alright". Nor can I say that "you won't have problems while inside". However, I can make your transition smoother by informing you on what to expect and how you can get through this.

It is my sincere hope and prayer that the things discussed in this book will help you and your family avoid some of the same trials and tribulations that I've been through. God speed friend. God speed.

01

Before you go

10 tasks you must complete before going to prison

Its mandatory that you handle all affairs and tie up any loose ends before going to prison. Hopefully, you're currently on bond/pretrial release, which will make "handling business" less complicated. For those reading this from a Federal Detention Center; you'll need some assistance from a loved one to accomplish the tasks listed in this chapter. The following is your "to do" list before you go:

TASK 1

The most important thing that you must do before you go is to **spend time with your family**.

If possible, go places and do things that you all enjoy. Spending quality time with your loved ones will take your mind off of your circumstances and give your family some great memories. *Be mindful to take plenty of pictures while spending time with your loved ones.* When you get to prison you'll be allowed to receive up to 20 pictures at a time through the mail. These pictures will bring you unexplainable joy. Trust me.

**If you're reading this from a federal detention center, try to visit with your family often while you're still close to home. According to policy, The Federal Bureau of Prisons has the right to send you to any institution within a 500 mile radius of your home. There's no guarantee that you'll end up in an institution nearby.*

TASK 2

Start an honest dialect with your spouse about what you expect from her/him during you absence. Questions like; "Can she/he tolerate "waiting" on you and "How does she/he feel about taking on your responsibilities". This conversation should be brutally honest! Regardless of the outcome, at least you'll have a better idea of what to expect from your spouse or significant other...........and even then things are still subject to change.

TASK 3

Start grooming others to take on you're responsibilities. Inform family members, friends, and business partners of what needs to be *done* to make things run smoothly in your absence. No issue is to small. Whether its keeping your light bill paid or making a business decision, someone has to act on your behalf.

*If you foresee ongoing issues that may require your signature, consider giving someone you trust power of attorney, so they can act on your behalf. ***Consult an attorney before doing this.***

TASK 4

Consider transferring ownership of your assets (cars, homes, bank accounts, etc) and selling off any assets you can't afford to keep. Especially if you'll be serving more than a year or two in prison. ***Consult an attorney before doing this.***

TASK 5

Set up an emergency fund that only you can touch. For example, you can use a Certificate of Deposit or another low risk investment vehicle. If you decide to invest in a Certificate of Deposit, set the maturity date to coincide with your release date.

** You never know what may happen during your time away. Hope for the best but always plan for rainy days.*

TASK 6

Contact debtors, lenders, and collection agencies that you cannot afford to continue paying. Explain your situation and if possible, try to come to some type of solution. It's not uncommon for inmates to get released to 40-50+ thousand dollars' worth of debt. Sometimes these debts could have been avoided.

TASK 7

Get a full physical. Especially if you have an existing medical condition, or you're on medication. Also, be sure to complete any necessary dental work. There's no guarantee you'll get the proper treatment. Trying to get dental work in federal prison is like "pulling teeth"! Seriously.

TASK 8

Be sure to bring your current medications and eyeglasses with you.

TASK 9

If you know which institution you're going to, visit www.bop.gov to find out specific information about your designation.

TASK 10

Set aside some cash to buy toiletries, clothing and food items from the prison commissary. Have someone wire this money to your inmate account one day after you arrive at the prison. Funds may be sent via western union using one of the following options:

- Go to the nearest western union and complete a Quick Collect form.
- Call 1-800-634-3422. To pay by credit/debit card.
- Or go to www.westernunion.com

**Sender must correctly provide inmate register number (Reg# 12345-678), and inmate name. Western union charges $9.95 for this service.*

Completing these 10 tasks before you go will help you and your family to avoid some of the trials and tribulations others' have faced before you. For those that can't get out on bond; you still want to complete as many of these tasks as possible while:

A) You're not too far from home

B) You still have people willing to help you out. It is a fact that loved ones are more willing to help you when you initially go to jail as opposed to later on down the line.

02

when you get there

Basic operations of the federal prison system

There are over 100 federal prisons in the US. So quite naturally each one operates slightly different. This chapter is your "heads up" on some of the things you'll initially experience within club fed.......regardless of which institution you go to.

1. CUSTODY LEVELS

Federal inmates are assigned a custody level *(high, medium, low, or minimum)* based on the following factors:

- Length of sentence
- Severity of crime
- Past criminal history
- Age

These factors combined determine whether you go to a "rough prison" or a "laid back" one. Below is an overview of the type of prison you'll end up at based on your custody level.

High Custody - This custody level is reserved for "lifers", the extremely violent, and career criminals. High custody inmates are sent to *United States Penitentiaries.* USP's have restricted movement 24 hours a day. Metal detectors can be found throughout the entire prison (even the library) to reduce the amount of homemade knives. Inmates are housed in 2 or 3 man cells. Overall, *USP's* are extremely dangerous. There's lots of violence, gangs, homosexuality, and plenty tension in the air.

Medium/High Custody - This custody level is also reserved for lifers, those with large amounts of time, the violent, and career criminals. Medium custody inmates are sent to *Federal Correctional Institutions.* FCI's have restricted movement 24 hours a day and there's metal detectors throughout the prison. There's not too much difference between an FCI and a USP; except for FCI's have less inmates serving life sentences. Inmates live in 2 or 3 man cells. These prisons are dangerous as well. Some violence, gangs, some homosexuality, and plenty of tension in the air.

Low Custody - This custody level is mostly for non violent offenders with 25 years or less. Inmates that fall into this custody are sent to low custody FCI's. Movement in these prisons isn't as restricted as medium and high custody. The living quarters are mostly open dormitories; similar to army barracks. Low custody FCI's aren't too dangerous. The gang presence isn't as heavy and you may see an occasional fight. But for the most part, these prisons are laid back.

Minimum Custody - This custody is designated for non-violent offenders with 10 years or less. Minimum custody inmates are sent to Federal Prison Camps. FPC inmates are allowed to freely move about the prison grounds during the day up until 9 or 10 at night. The living quarters are open dorms; similar to army barracks. The overall atmosphere at a camp is very relaxed. You will rarely see a fight and the majority of these facilities don't even have fences. If one must do prison time, it's best to spend it at an FPC.

2. ORIENTATION

When you initially get to prison, you must go through a 2-5 day orientation phase. Orientation consists of several staff members(and possibly a few inmates) informing you of the institution procedures, rules, and inmate rights/privileges.

Be mindful to listen closely during orientation. Violating institutional rules may result in loss of privileges or worse- loss of ***good time.*** ** *Federal inmates must serve a total of 87% of their sentences. Which equals out to about 10 ½ months served on each year. The month and a half that you don't serve is called **good time.** Each day of good time lost is another day that you will have to spend in prison.*

3. VISITATION

Most federal institutions allow inmates to have contact visitation. Which means you are able to physically touch your family. Visitation hours and/or days are limited and will vary depending on which institution you're at.

4. WORK

Each inmate is required to work, or go to school (if you don't have a high school diploma). Job availability in prison is usually limited to teaching/tutoring, plumbing, electricians, welders, orderlies, kitchen workers(*cooks, bakers, dishwashers*), and recreational workers(referees, coaches, and scorekeepers).

You'll have the opportunity to choose where you would like to work. Most of the jobs only require about an hour or two of actual work per day. Below is the hourly pay scale for an inmate worker.

Grade 1	0.40 per hour
Grade 2	0.29 per hour
Grade 3	0.17 per hour
Grade 4	0.12 per hour
Grade 5	$5.25 (once a per month)

5. PHONE TIME

Inmates are allowed 300 minutes of phone time each month. At the time of this writing phone calls cost 0.23 per minute.

6. EMAIL

The Bureau of Prisons has introduced an email system that allows inmates to send and receive text based messages. No images. Email time is unlimited and costs' 0.05 per minute.

7. COMMISSARY

Each institution operates a commissary that sells various food items, cosmetics, and clothing. Inmates are permitted to spend a maximum of 290.00 per month on commissary. **Commissary items; like stamps, tuna fish, and mackerel are used as currency amongst inmates for: goods(extra food from the kitchen) and services(haircuts and clothes ironed).*

8. UNIT TEAMS

Upon arrival, inmates are assigned a counselor and a case manager. They will be directly responsible for overseeing your "rehabilitation" and addressing any day to day questions/issues you may have.

9. FINES

The payment process for court costs and/or fines will automatically be initiated during incarceration. Unit teams will set up a minimum payment plan for inmates to pay fines.

03

Your safety

Avoiding conflicts while doing time

Your first week or two in prison will probably be **THE** most stressful part of your entire stay. Thoughts of whether you'll be safe or not will often cross your mind.

Usually, it takes about a week or so to realize that most of the "worst case scenarios" you had in mind were just figments of your imagination. Before you know it, you'll be making acquaintances and blending in with everyone else. Which is a good thing........just don't get *too* comfortable. All the awful things that we hear about happening in prison(conflict with staff, extortion, fights, homosexuality, and murder) these things really do happen. However, 99% of the time, people bring these situations on themselves. Certain behaviors *always, always, always* cause problems in prison. Fortunately, you'll have the benefit of knowing what causes problems before you get there. Be mindful of the following:

- *Minding your own business* – When you get to prison, you will certainly see other inmates breaking the rules and doing things that are flat out disgusting! However, I strongly suggest that you *act* as if you don't see anything. Especially if the situation doesn't directly affect you. Let the staff do their jobs. You don't want other inmates to feel as if you're an informant. Being labeled as an informant will make your prison stay miserable. Staff members will try to convince you that its alright to report any wrong that you *see*. But always remember that the staff goes home after their 8 hour shifts are over. Yet you'll still have to live with the people they want you to turn in.
- *Gambling* – Do not gamble in prison!!!! Whether its a card game or a simple sporting event. For some reason when money is on the line, it causes too much confusion. A few bucks may be meaningless to you, but to the next person it may mean the world.
- *Homosexuality* – The chances of one getting raped in federal prison is almost slim to none. In fact, 99% of the homosexual activity in federal prisons consist of two "willing participants".

  Each prison will have a handful of "openly gay" individuals and a bunch of "down-low gay" individuals. The "down-low gays" always out number the "openly gays" which always causes problems and lots of confusion. To give you a better understanding of this situation, just imagine being in a city where men outnumber the women. Or women outnumber the men. The confusion and problems will stem from scarcity.

- *T. V's* – Do not turn the televisions or make suggestions about what channels to watch. There are individuals in prison that have nothing better to do than to guard "their TV" 24/7. These inmates will gladly argue or fight you for "disrespecting" their territory. If you enjoy watching television, simply pull up a chair and watch. If you don't like whats on, move on!
- *Horse playing/coarse joking* – Do not get into the habit of playing and joking. You never know when someones having a bad day. Or you may be having one yourself. If you open the door for this type of behavior; other inmates will expect you to play and joke all the time.
- *Staff interaction* – When interacting with staff, always be mindful of your tone, choice of words, and body language. Even when you don't agree with the things they say and do. If a staff member "perceives" you to be aggressive, disrespectful, or rebellious; they will make your prison stay a whole lot tougher than it has to be. Also, basic physical contact such as hand shakes, pats on the back, and of course hugs is strictly prohibited.
- *Revealing personal information* – Be extremely cautious when discussing your personal business (court issues, financial info, family info, etc.) There are many trustworthy individuals in prison, but you can never fully know what a persons motives are.
- *Personal space* – Federal prisons are overcrowded. Each inmate has a small amount of space(about the size of a small bathroom in most cases) to sleep and store personal belongings. Be mindful not to invade others' space. Some inmates get very possessive and will fight

over small things such as "who can sit at a certain table". Before you start getting into a daily routine, be observant of what other inmates are already doing. If you're not sure about what you should do in regards to invading someones space; simply ask. Common courtesy will take you a long way.

- *Borrowing things from others* – Do not accept or borrow things from just any body in prison; with the exception of *The Christian Community*. Usually there will be some Christians brothers or sisters that provide new inmates with basic toiletries to get through those first few nights. Its okay to accept their hospitality. Other than that, I suggest that you be extremely cautious of accepting anything from other inmates.
- *Angry/Bitter people* – There are people in prison that spend their time bickering and complaining about their circumstances. These inmates are like a cancer and they try to destroy others' hopes, dreams, and accomplishments with their negativity. You'll quickly discover who the "angry people" are. Go the opposite direction.

04

Your health

Maintaining physical, mental, and spiritual health

Its very easy to become physically, mentally, and even spiritually ill in a prison environment. You'll be living in close quarters among individuals that have health/hygiene issues, psychological problems, and strange religious beliefs. All of which make it very easy to catch a disease, become mentally stressed, or stray from your faith. With that being said, I strongly suggest that you monitor the following aspects of your health:

PHYSICAL HEALTH

Its mandatory that you take care of your body as best as possible while doing time. The better your physical health; the more efficient your immune system will be at fighting off all the sicknesses floating around. You won't be able to depend on the medical care provided by the institution. They usually recommend Ibuprofen for every ailment. The only solution for taking care of your body is to eat healthy and exercise consistently. Which is fairly easy to do in prison. Alcohol and rich foods are basically non-existent, and one has more than enough time to hit the gym or participate in recreational activities such as basketball, handball, softball,etc. Find something physical that you enjoy and just "do it".

MENTAL/EMOTIONAL HEALTH

Doing prison time is more of a mental/emotional challenge than anything else. If you're unstable in this area; 1 month *in* will feel like 1 year.! Many of the day to day issues like being away from family, constant noise, shakedowns (searches), and the way staff and inmates treat you can lead to plenty of stress and/or frustration. In most cases; there's no recourse for the things that bother you in prison. Which can cause frustration to turn into anger or possibly rage.

Dealing with stress in prison can be difficult, but its doable. Many inmates find solace through visitation with family, exercise, meditation, prayer, reading, writing, arts/crafts, sports and board games. Professional psychology services are also available to to help inmates deal with a variety of mental and emotional issues. The key to not getting stressed out is to simply find as many "constructive" avenues to vent as you possibly can.

SPIRITUAL HEALTH

The Federal Bureau of Prisons gives each inmate the opportunity to practice any religion he/she chooses. Which in my opinion, is a blessing and a curse. On one hand, this religious freedom gives believers the opportunity to "worship the Father in Spirit and truth" (John 4:23-24). Yet on the other hand, that same religious freedom allows inmates to practice witchcraft and many other false doctrines. These false religions can cause unbelievers and those that are "weak in faith" to stray even further away from The True Living God. With that being said, make every effort to maintain your spiritual health. Constantly be on guard for those that try to introduce you to false religions and doctrines. Spiritual health and growth can only be obtained by:

- Reading/studying The Bible
- Fellow-shipping with other believers
- Praying

Its that simple.

05

Your relationships

Insights for keeping your relationships intact

A prison sentence is difficult for the individual that has to serve the time. But, believe it or not, its just as hard (if not harder) on the family, friends, and associated that get left behind. Especially if you're the "breadwinner" or the "glue" that holds everyone together.

Incarceration creates a type of ripple effect that will impact the strength of all your relationships. A few of your relationships will grow stronger as a result of this situation. Yet some of your relationships will become strained, distant, or simply fall apart. Your goal is to try to keep as many of your relationships intact while doing time.

Strong relationships are built on good communication. However, communication avenues for federal inmates is limited to *visitation, phone, email and regular mail.*

- *Visitation* – inmates are allowed roughly 8-14 visits per month; depending on custody levels. Physical contact during visitation is limited to *one kiss and embrace upon arrival* and one more *kiss and embrace at the end of the visit.* No sex allowed. Not even for married couples. Each visit is monitored by a correctional officer.
- *Phones* – phone time is limited to 300 minutes per month(400 during November and December for the holidays). Inmates have to wait (30min.-1 hour) after each call before placing another. Each call is limited to 15 minutes and phones are shut off from 11pm-6am. Calls are monitored and recorded.
- *Email* – although email minutes are basically unlimited, incoming/outgoing emails are "held" for an hour after you or your loved ones hit the send button. Emails are also monitored and recorded.
- *Regular mail* – regular mail is limited to letters, books, magazines and pictures(maximum of 20 pictures at a time). All incoming/outgoing mail is read and searched.

With only 4 means of communication and numerous limitations communicating with loved ones will oftentimes get frustrating. There will be times that you feel as if you're in a long-distance relationship with everyone you know- even your kids. Nevertheless, you'll have to make the most of the situation if you want to keep your relationships intact. Below are some insights that others before you have used to keep their **various relationships** strong while they did time:

- ***Wife/husband*** – its very possible to keep a marital bond strong throughout a prison sentence. However, its going to take compromise, patience, forgiveness, understanding, trust, honest communication, and a whole lot of love. Its also important to keep in mind that the "free spouse" is doing time too; just in a different way. You'll be in prison physically while your other half is doing time mentally and emotionally.

  When communicating with your significant other from prison, do everything in your power to encourage, uplift, and comfort her/him. Avoid petty arguments; such as pointing out what they are doing wrong. Instead, find ways to congratulate your spouse on what their doing well. You want your spouse to look forward to communicating with you.

- ***Children*** – keeping strong bonds with your children will be largely dependent on the relationship you have with the other parent or caregiver. If you're on good terms with the other parent you'll automatically increase the likelihood of your children writing you, accepting your calls, and their willingness to visit with you.

  Communicate with your kids on a consistent basis. For example: call, send mail, and/or emails on the same days each week.; whether they respond back or not. In this way you'll make your presence felt and they will know you're constantly thinking of them.

***FYI:** *statistics show that children (especially teenaged boys) that are separated from a parent due to incarceration are 50-*

60% more likely to go to prison themselves. I can personally confirm this statistic. While I was serving my prison sentence, my teenaged son went to jail *twice!* So, with that being said, I urge you to monitor your children's behavior as close as possible while doing your time and afterwards.

- **Family** – regardless of what happens in this life, we only get one family. We might not always agree with our family members but their still family nonetheless. With that being said, reach out to as many family members as possible during your incarceration. Communicate with those willing to communicate with you. And do your best not to hold old grudges. Life is too short.
- **Friends** – a prison sentence will give you an opportunity to see who's really in your corner and who's not. Your true friends will stick by you to the best of their abilities. While on the other hand, some of those you "consider" to be friends will quickly let you down. In any case, try to learn from this experience so you can choose friends more wisely in the future.

  Keep in contact with your *true friends*. It won't take long to discover who they are. Also, communicate with those willing to communicate with you........ as long as its a *positive* relationship.
- **Business partners** – If you're an owner or partner of a business that will continue operating; you will definitely need to stay in contact with those that are picking up your slack. The only issue that you'll face here is that federal inmates are not allowed to *"personally operate a business"*. This rule is strictly enforced by guards that monitor inmates' phone calls, letters, and

emails. Inmates are allowed to communicate and give business related *advice* to a business partner. However, one cannot give orders, write checks, receive business mail, or anything of that nature.

I suggest that you stay in close contact with your business partners. Just be mindful to communicate within the prison rules.

06

Making the most of your time

Education opportunities in prison

Furthering your education while incarcerated will help make the most of the time as well as decrease your chances of ever coming back. If you gain nothing else from being "locked up"; at least walk away wiser than before you came. If you don't gain wisdom from this situation; all the hardships you and your family go through will be in vain.

There are numerous opportunities to learn something new or teach others what you already know. One just has to be willing to *think outside the box*. The following are some educational avenues that one can pursue while doing time. **One of the avenues mentioned in this chapter can possibly get a whole year taken off of your sentence.* **See residential drug abuse program.**

GED –GED classes are mandatory for any inmate that doesn't have a high school diploma. No exceptions.

Vocational Training – each institution has an education department that offers vocational type courses to prepare inmates for life on the outside. The options and quality of these courses will vary depending which institution you're at. I've seen everything from Microsoft Office courses to forklift training. In some cases, inmates receive official certifications from accredited organizations or community colleges. Each institution will usually offer 3 or more vocational courses free of charge.

Residential Drug Abuse Program – RDAP is a 500 hour (9½ month) substance abuse course that inmates can take and receive up to one year off of their sentence. Anyone can take this program, however, to receive the time off one **must** meet the following criteria:

- Must have documented history of alcohol/drug abuse 12 months prior to incarceration. The most acceptable documentation is the ***Pre-sentencing report***. Be sure to let your pre-sentencing officer know that you have a drinking or drug problem-*even if you don't think you have a problem*. The **PSR** will be sent to the prison you'll be designated to and this will be the only documentation you need to get time off.
- Can **not** have a two level enhancement for a firearm or use of a methamphetamine lab in your instant offense.
- Must be able to speak some English
- Must have 16 months or more to receive sentence reduction.

I strongly suggest that anyone coming into the federal prison system take the Residential Drug Abuse Program. Even if you don't meet the criteria for a sentence reduction. This program deals with a lot of issues outside the scope of drug and alcohol abuse. This program takes an extensive look at criminal thinking and teaches how to live a balanced life. In my opinion, this was one of the best programs that I took during my incarceration. It also had the greatest impact on my life as well.

Law library – a computerized law library is available for those that want to do legal research. This is a priceless resource if you're appealing your case or trying to become more *aware* of the federal laws and guidelines.

Correspondence courses – inmates are allowed to take college courses and/or certification programs by mail. However, The Federal Bureau of Prisons does **not** promote or provide information about correspondence courses, nor will it pay for this educational avenue. Federal inmates must take it upon themselves to seek out and finance correspondence courses.

There are a number of colleges that allow students to attend by mail. A great place to start is by doing a Google search for ***"accredited colleges by mail"*** . Its very possible to find a degree program that's suitable for you. You can find courses on everything from business to theology.

"How to books" – if your crime stemmed from the occupation you were in (like most federal inmates), chances are you'll have to find another way to earn a living. "How to books" are excellent resources to seek out alternative career opportunities. If you have an idea about which career direction you want to go in; I guarantee you can find a "how to" book for that career/business venture. Example books: internet business, vending machines, dollar stores, wholesale merchant, day trading, information brokering.

Trade related/business publications – subscribing to publications related to your profession is an excellent way to stay updated on new developments in your field. Examples include, entrepreneur magazine, Inc. magazine, and wall street journal.

Teach a class/tutor – if you have specialized knowledge on a subject that could benefit other inmates, you may be allowed to teach what you know in a classroom setting. Teaching others will keep you mind sharp as well as give you an opportunity to help someone else.

Learn another language – foreigners (especially Latino) make up a large portion of the population in federal prisons. Foreign languages are often taught in classroom settings, and its fairly easy to find someone willing to teach you one on one.

Learn to play an instrument – most institutions will provide instruments for inmate use. Usually keyboards, drums, pianos, and guitars. Learning to play an instrument can be therapeutic and help pass lots of time.

Write a book – if you're the creative type or you simply have the ability to write well; you could easily write a book/s during your prison stay. Doing time offers the perfect set of circumstances for a writer. Trust me. The book you're reading at this moment was authored a few months before I was released!

***If you have an idea you need help getting out on paper or you need advice on where to start; feel free to contact me at: mackwayne1980@gmail.com*

07

when its over

Halfway house, home confinement, and supervised release

Whether you're doing 10 months or several years, as long as you have a "reasonable release date" you'll make it back into society one day. The following is what you can expect to experience towards the end of your sentence.

Federal inmates are required to spend the last 2-6 months of their sentences in a *halfway house* or on *home confinement*. To give you an idea of how this works, lets say for example you receive a 24 month sentence. Its mandatory that you serve 87% of that (if no reductions are involved), which is 20 months. Out of those 20 months, at least 2-6 months will be served in a halfway house or on home confinement.

Halfway houses are an extension of federal prison. All the same rules, yet with a lot more privileges. Halfway houses allow inmates to work (up to 55 hours per week), attend school, and go on home passes for the weekend.

Inmates are required to pay 25% of all gross income (unless disabled) for the privilege of residing in the halfway house. Which is a small price to pay for the amount of freedom you'll have. The primary purpose of halfway houses is to give inmates an opportunity to gradually transition back into society. ***If at all possible, try to secure employment* ***before leaving prison.*** *Inmates who have or find a job immediately upon arrival to the halfway house will have many more privileges, and are eligible for weekend passes and home confinement.*

Home confinement is just what it sounds like- you're *confined* to your home. In general, inmates are initially sent to a halfway house *before* being allowed to go on home confinement. However, its very possible to leave directly from prison to serve your last 2-6 months at your home. Inmates sent to home confinement are monitored by phone and in some instances by electronic ankle monitor. While on home confinement, inmates are still required to pay 25% of all gross income.

Supervised release is mandatory for all federal inmates. At sentencing, the judge will specify a certain amount of supervised release (probation),which ranges anywhere from 2-10 years. The supervised release portion of a federal sentence isn't activated until you're officially released from halfway house custody. At that time, you will have a certain amount of hours to report to a federal probation officer and he/she will inform you on what they expect. For the most part, federal PO's are fairly reasonable people; as long as you do what you're supposed to do. Generally, while on federal probation you are required to:

- Meet all court ordered obligations, such as fines, restitution, child support, community services, and substance abuse classes.
- Call in a specified amount of times per week and submit to random drug testing.
- Not commit any crimes or associate with known felons.
- Notifying the officer if you plan to leave the county or state for any reason.
- Fill out monthly report before making any major purchases.

Violation of any of these stipulations will result in more prison time. ***FYI:** it is possible to get your supervised release terminated early if you consistently do everything required of you. Simply ask you probation officer to find out the necessary procedures.

After thought

After serving 12 years in federal prison, I can't help but look at life through "optimistic eyes". While others see lack, I see abundance. And while others are saying "it" can't be done, I'm looking for ways to make "it" possible. Yeah, I completely understand that doing time can be a very bad situation. However, I've witnessed many strong willed individuals learn from their prison experience and go on to live very productive lives.

I'm at the point now where I **know** everything in life happens for a reason. Including what ***I*** went through and what ***you're*** going through right now. Both blessings and hardships come from God (Lamentations 3 v 37-40), and everything that happens to us has some type of purpose in our lives.

My friend, always remember that God has a way of using tough situations to get our attention so we can become the people He has called us to be. I encourage you to do your best to discover what God is trying to show **you** in *this* situation.

Hopefully the contents of this book answered any questions or concerns you may have had. If not, feel free to contact me at: **mackwayne1980@gmail.com**

Made in the USA
Monee, IL
04 November 2026

67388648R20030